Also by Cliff Forshaw

Satyr   (Shoestring Press, 2017)

Pilgrim Tongues   (Wrecking Ball, 2015)

Vandemonian   (Arc, 2013)

Trans   (The Collective Press, Wales, 2005)

RE:VERB

Cliff Forshaw

ISBN: 978-1-915079-85-5

Cover designed by Aaron Kent

Edited and typeset by Aaron Kent

Broken Sleep Books Ltd
Rhydwen,
Talgarreg,
SA44 4HB
Wales

Contents

For Simon Thom, old friend and fellow Rimbaud enthusiast.

RE:VERB

or Rimbaud's Terrestrial Adventure: echoes from a life in three parts

Cliff Forshaw

1. BOHO / HOBO

Hooligan in Hell 1871-73

...Once, if I remember well,
my life was a feast where all the wines flowed free.
So, how come I did my time in Hell?

... Well... I sat Beauty on my knee;
found her bitter, slapped her fucking face.
(Not proud: just saying how I came to be

the Laureate of this damned odd place.)
I railed about how she'd flirted, lied.
– Too late, I get it now, her hidden grace.

That silly pretty thing had failed, but tried.
Pity... I now know how to greet that girl.
You know the one. Beauty. The one who died.

My inheritance? Just this: bad blood;
the inept Gauls left me my pale-blue eyes;
no noble marble pile, just pitch, thatch, wood;
idolatry, sacrilege, my love of lies.

And Foolish Virgin to my Infernal Groom,
that prurient slap-head, self-pitying whingeing pain,
all gloomy lust and sanctimonious doom;
so weak and lyric, so viciously... *Verlaine.*

The Master of maudlin lust and drunken rants,
prick and a crucifix popping out of his pants.

Then, tail between his legs, shit-scared of life,
he's pissed off back to the childlike pregnant wife.

Gave him something to whisper, that much at least,
into the hairy ear of his greasy priest.

*

In *salles d'attente*, locked in, we dossed
with drunken madmen who screamed and tossed
themselves to sleep. V cadged odd francs
to smoke and piss away. We stank.

In Brussels once, when angry, pissed,
he fucking shot me through the wrist,
accidentally fired again... He missed.

> *I remember the sling around my arm,*
> *(I held his hand once – gently, calm –*
> *and jammed a knife right through his palm).*

Two years' hard labour for the sod.
Inside, he got that taste for God.

> *(Wasn't the first time I'd cut up rough:*
> *angelic, but filthy, ragged, tough,*
> *at the* Bonshommes Vilains, *in my old hobnailed boots,*
> *I mocked the bohemians, the dandies, the suits.*
>
> *And bored with the verse of some tedious turd,*
> *I end-stopped each line out-loud with a "MERDE!"*
> *Carjat protested and called me a lout,*
> *demanded Verlaine had me thrown out.*
>
> *I stood up and mocked this poetaster's limp prick,*
> *and stuck him pig-like with V's handy sword-stick.)*

Alchemy of the Word

But also...
>A Hermes Trismegistus, unseen, unheard,
>>I conjured the Alchemy of the Word;
>deciphered fragments of the vowels' spectrum,
>>my mind a wand, a bow, a plectrum.
>I struck the rainbow's neurasthenic strings,
>>plumbed all tenebrous, timbrous things.
>Then, when sounding out riddles as Gnostic songs,
>>it came to me: *I was going wrong.*

Sortilege and Thaumaturgy,
Hermeneutics, Oneiromancy,
Almanacs, O Dark Abraxas,
Orphic Devotees, Eleusis,
Epiphanic Hocus-Pocus,
Diabolic Psychomancy,

Tantra, Sutra, Old Grimoires,
Transits of Venus, Mercury, Mars,
Cabbalistic Hierophants,
Mumbo-Jumbo, Obeah, Cant,
Hoodoo-Voodoo, Occult Muse,
Esoteric Marabouts.

>From such Fiendish Tomes I busked the Blues,
>>left a hobo chorus of cryptic clues.
>But my *rational* derangement of all the senses
>>(shamanically ancient, prophetically new)
>left me wondering: Who was the densest,
>>Poet or Reader? I got no reviews.

Still, gleaming minarets shone proud
of workhouse chimneys which belched black clouds;
a squad of angels often drummed
as I stole through Europe. And, yes, I bummed.

To reinvent both Life and Love
– I'd reunite that long-lost pair.
While devils in puddles mocked sky up above
I dried my soul in the crime-thick air.

I staged myself at dull first-nights,
smug poets' eyes were my footlights.
And through the kaleidoscopic lens
of boozers, music-halls, opium dens,
I put the gate-crashed world to rights:
salon soirées – more drunken fights.

"Take eloquence and break its neck!"

...So V declaimed, but still wrote dreck.
He aimed for music not "rhetoric",
but with tooth too sweet and ear too sick,
he ladled that gloopy syrup on thick.

While I became a fabulous opera,
his verse got worse – pious, soppier.
If he's remembered it's for that quote;
but on seas of booze, as our lives got choppier,
he lacked sea-legs for my Drunken Boat.
Several times, I'd cast off, leave
at the erratic tiller of my *Bateau ivre*.

> *Real life is absent!* Or *absinthe*, at least;
> the Emerald Fairy's wand can damn,
> but he who makes of himself a Beast,
> forgets the pain of being a man.

Those poetasters feasting with panthers
sucked bee-like from *Les Fleurs du Mal*:
stanzas all stamens with pollen-filled anthers,
their verses satanic, or piggish, unholy,
left snoring by Circe from snuffling her Moly.

Parnassians chiselled stone, bright-Greek,
their verses formal, strict, sun-dappled.
The Bohos lacked rigour, ear or technique,
but, snouting the dirt for worm-rotten apples,
confuddled by booze or the somnolent poppy,
they took Baudelaire and botched up a copy.

While they were getting stoned or pissed
– so was I – but this was Quest.
I mapped the soul like an Alienist,
Subject: myself. I ran the tests,
analysed each dawn's raw data.
Of course, I fooled myself; you guessed.
I realised this, only so much later.

I is another

I gulped down poisons, the spirits came;
damned angels spoke God's secret Names:
Insomnia, Delirium, Psychic Violence;
I kept my own counsel: *The Master of Silence.*

I thought I'd cracked the secret Code,
broken that Cipher, withheld the Key,
but I'd just trekked, not mapped, that road.
Je est un autre: I fled from *me.*

> *As for l'Alchimie du Verbe?*
> *The Verb did nothing. The Word was sick.*
> *I'd forced its throat, poured in my purge.*
> *But no emetic could do that trick.*
> *I quit: a quack, no thaumaturge.*
> **Re: Verb. Reverb. Reverb. Reverb.**

To possess the truth in one soul, one flesh?
Dead end. Rethink. Now start afresh!

> *Of that life I led, those things I wrote,*
> *what echoes now's* **Je est un autre.**
> *That much, at least, remains still true:*
> *to everyone, I've always thought,*
> *several other lives were due.*
> *That Seer was dead, the time was right:*
> *be someone else, find sun, heat, light.*

Adieu

Then quit that path to trek, my pipe gripped tight,
the only sound for miles, hobnails on lanes.
Just like before, but I no longer write.
Boots, then boats, odd carts, more boots, freight trains.
I'm someone else, elsewhere, *elsewho*. In flight.
Forget Baudelaire's famously amoral twin,
I am Legion, all the quarrelling multitudes within.

And I *is always alien,* Other:
alter egos, devils, brothers.
I shift my shape and twist my tongue
right through each new strange land or region;
ventriloquise each migratory song.
I am many, a Foreign Legion:
an engineer; a merchant-trader.
I play each part: a masquerader.

Don't know how I even thought, e.g.
that soldiering was the life for me.
There was the Dutch Colonial Army:
joined up, was double-quick shipped out
to Java and standing to attention,
much tedious stuff not worth the mention
– the military, the military,
it never quite worked out for me.

I just took off, tramped right through the jungle,
found a port, a false ID.
For weeks I worked my passage back.
For weeks and weeks, I'm all at sea.

Deserter, barman, docker. Me?
I'm labourer, linguist, foreman, tout.
I spend a season on a building site,
lose my rag, and find a fight.
They're in my face. They swear and shout.
Time to split, to get right out.
On the road, down on my luck.
Time again to get the fuck
Out! Out! Out! Out!

*

Alone, I hold the key to this wild parade,
its terrifying voices, repulsive masks.
I don the grotesque finery of trade.
to learn each secret craft, perform its tricks.
A carnival of one, fresh from the road,
I doss in castles, barracks, I haunt the sticks.

As for Literature, let me report
there's no outstanding business there for me.
That account is cleared. Those battles fought.
Long since I left Opinion's petty court.
I am a multitude. Each one is free.

*

Years pass by. The countries too.
To everyone, it seemed to me,
several other lives were due.
I am as rootless as the wandering Jew,
resolve into adieu, a dew, a dew.

*

2. AFRICA

"A strapping fellow with an intelligent, energetic look about him."
— Bardey, Rimbaud's boss in Aden

In Alexandria, there was no work.
Set sail for Cyprus. Bullshit, but not to worry,
I'm hard-but-fair, the foreman in a quarry.
I keep an eye, make sure they graft, don't shirk.
Course, there's always one who tries it on.
Don't take that bad-mouth back-chat. Should I be sorry
I threw the rock that cracked that bastard's head?
He fell. Sparked out. His gang was mean, but stunned.
I left him there stone-cold. Not *for*, but really dead.
Don't hang about. Too fast for getting caught,
I'm gone. What could I do, but get the fuck
double-quick down to Limassol, the port?
Got rowed out to a leaving ship. Pot-luck.
End up in Aden, hinge of Empires, stuck.

*

Dark Continent by cart, horse, camel, dhow.
– I'll be absolutely modern now:

a practical, read-the-market sort of Seer.
– Could raise a son to be an engineer.

A Man of Science, with instruments and charts.
– I'll trade: sell coffee, ivory, mechanical parts.

Time to hunt down that real but absent Life.
– Have money. Power. Servants. A dark-skinned wife.

I watch the caravans, all fully-laden,
arrive and leave where East meets West in Aden.

There's opportunity here. I'll make the most.
– Just got a job at Bardey's trading post.

Harar

The more adventurous Abyssinian travellers [...] attempted Harar, but attempted in vain. The bigoted ruler and barbarous people threatened death to the Infidel who ventured within their walls.
— *Sir Richard Burton,* First Footsteps in East Africa; or, An Exploration of Harar, *1856*

A rock without a single blade of grass,
Aden is nothing but lava, sand and shit.
Those sweating lime-kiln months impressed the boss.
Then fresh! my dhow sea-breezed across the Straits.

Took camel drivers; whipped shape into that caravan.
Fully-loaded, the twenty-odd day desert plod,
then high along the cool Somali plain.
Round here, they'd murdered Bardey's other man.

The huddled night, a goat-haunch spitting on the fire,
we listened for marauders, posted guards
against the ever-vengeful raiding tribes,
hyenas howling under the shivering stars.

Three weeks: red ochre atop a ridge – Harar:
the walls are ancient but in poor repair.
Egyptian sentries at the "Gate of Conquests",
a shaky garrison at their empire's edge.

Show the letter from Governor Nadi Pasha,
pass through the walls at Bab el F'touh
into the once forbidden Holy City.
– A slum. This is no Timbuktoo.

*

Odd stumpy minarets, the houses squat;
mud-huts with scraggy sycamores for shade.
Castrated slaves in the market-place (though Egypt
signed the British pact to ban the trade).

Not long ago, they'd put all Infidels to death,
till Raouf Pasha took the city, killed the Emir.
With the troops came these Armenians and Greeks,
set stalls where old men sit and chew their *khat*.

The company house is near the *maidan*; Bardey
left his assistant Pichard here in charge.
At six they shut the gates against the night.
We hear hyenas howl inside and out.

> *(We live next door to the stinking slaughterhouse,*
> *our doors kept shut to prevent a visit from*
> *the town's de facto sanitation service.)*

Things change. The city is opening up for trade.
Africa now flows through Suez; Red Sea ports
ship Abyssinian coffee, spices, skins.
The merchants come, old hierarchies fade.

Here's Africa's Horn of Plenty, and Harar's the key
to this cornucopia. Soon, the *Barr Adjam*,
the Land Beyond, will open too. The game's
afoot: Great Britain, France, now Italy...

Both in the town and hereabouts I see
the future, waiting for a man like me.

*

He's off, Mahomedan-like in turban,
gone trading hides and ivory, or,
camels loaded with his newly-ordered
state-of-the-art assorted instruments,
pointing exploratory expeditions
through sullen villages, wastelands
with their rumours of marauding tribes,
into the parts as yet unmapped.

*

Head Office

Aden, again, January 1883

I saw the future: could be the coming man.
Somehow it hasn't quite worked out to plan.

I'd been there a year, and though often ill,
had got to learn the trade and oiled the wheels,

explored the territory towards the Ogaden;
had plans for other expeditions when

Bardey called me back to head office here.
Now, it's already another wasted year

of kicking my heels, stuck in Aden again.
I plot and plan. Like mice. Like other men.
I ask myself: *And if not now, then when?*

Incident

Aden, spring 1883

Tensions lately rising among the workers;
came to a sudden head down in the warehouse.

Ali Shamok was extremely insolent.
I permitted myself to give him a light slap.
Very light, no more, a little tap.

The coolies, together with certain Arabs present,
grabbed hold of me. He struck me in the face,
ripped my shirt and violently brandished a stick.

Since then he's lodged a complaint with the police
– he falsely claims I threatened him with a knife.
He lies to poison my case, incite the natives.

Bardey has now dismissed this troublemaker
and spoken to the Consul. The case is settled
but a bad taste remains... and enemies here.

The boss is sending me to Harar again;
I'll be in charge this time. And out of Aden.

Rimbaud?

those Harar conversations

Few got the better of *Abdo Rimbo.*
His practice, maybe, could be a little sharp;
he knew his market, how to wheel and deal.
Took his chances. Fingered every pie.
By far the region's most important trader.

You need it, he's the go-to middle man:
coffee, cloth, and not afraid of guns,
I know King Menelik relied on him.
Meticulous accounts. A man of vision:
he saw the future, knew the bottom line.

"A contented misanthrope," I've heard it said;
"self-sufficient" with his little household:
his long-time servant, Djami; the local girl.
The sort of man who has settled into his world.

*

He kept himself much to himself;
though often curt, I've seen him charm,
tell witty stories in company.
Of all the businessmen out there,
many thought him by far the best.
How was it that he did so well?
The man was trusted. Kept his word

*

"And did you know that Rimbaud wrote?"
... Oh, yes, some very fine reports
for the *Société de Géographie*;

some talk of a book on Abyssinia.
He set it down, precise, first class:
terrain, the tribes, the languages.

He was, of course, the first to report
from personal experience of the Ogaden:
extremely interesting observations
... a very valuable account despite its dryness.
A fine analytical mind, but no poet.
No, no-one could accuse Rimbaud of that.

He covered it all: ethnographic detail
on tribes we'd never heard of, much less seen;
flora, fauna, climate, topography.
It's all in his *Rapport sur L'Ogadine.*

I was impressed, and passed it on.
Imagine, a mere company report
published by the *Société de Géographie.*

I believe the *Société* wrote to ask permission
to include him in its series – imagine this! –
of famous geographers and explorers.
It seems he never answered their request.

*

M. Rimbaud? I'm sure he reads the papers
when he can, and keeps an eye on things.
Talk was he'd gained some fame in Paris
– "a legendary figure for the *Symbolistes.*"
Can't see it myself. There may be other Rimbauds.
Must be someone else.

And even if, well he's long done with that,
some youthful folly he can't shake off.
He's now *un homme d'affaires – très sérieux.*

He sees the shifts of empires, has words in ears,
acts as an agent in every sense.

*

There is a man, Rembau, some say "Rambon",
– one of the cleverest, most active agents of the French
in those regions bordering British influence,
... and, with the Italian toehold in Eritrea....
They turn a blind eye to his other interests.

You ask if he's involved with slaves? Out here,
that's an Arab trade – no European
would dare upset the Abou Bekr clan.
Of course, no white man trading here can keep
his hands entirely clean. ...Well, as for guns...

*

Gun-running
Autumn 1885

Of the ten or so whites in Shoa
      (and all were running guns),
Monsieur Labatut up in Ankober
      was piling up the funds.

Well, King Menelik the Second,
      he liked this Labatut:
and His Highness the Shoan warlord
      gave him land and servants too.

Seems the Frenchman was sitting pretty,
      married *à la africaine;*
arms-dealer by Royal Appointment
      – Menelik's go-to, can-do man.

But he needed a business partner
      who could handle a caravan,
someone to shlep the guns and stop
      the shit from hitting the fan.

Rimbaud had a reputation
      as a trader who knew the land,
from the highlands down to the Red Sea coast,
      like the back of his leathery hand.

Well, Arthur was an ambitious man,
      you could say he had an itch,
for another kind of venture that
      would make him filthy rich.

When Bardey tried to warn him
      from getting in too deep,
then Rimbaud broke with his old boss
      – without losing any sleep.

Rimbaud at Tadjourah, 1886

... the goods are concealed under tents... Twenty stalwart Abyssinians, very well-disciplined and armed with Remingtons, are constantly ready to rally round at the slightest alarm.... We also visited another of our compatriots, M. Rimbaud, who had been striving to get his means of transport together for the past three months. The Sultan agreed to come to his assistance, but not without first exacting baksheesh.
— *Dr L. Faurot, May 1886*

The rifles got sequestered,
      petty functionaries froze the trade;
I poured baksheesh in their machinations.
      - Christ! I almost prayed.

Even so, I've kicked my dusty heels
      for eleven months and more.
This plan to make me filthy rich
      just keeps me here and poor.

I saw Rimbaud at Tadjourah,
      tall, greying, rather gaunt.
He wore a skull-cap like a local,
      knew all the native haunts.

The other traders camped and left;
      I thought he'd never leave,
though he always gave the sense that he
      had something up his sleeve.

Backhanders, sweeteners, kickbacks, bungs:
      the wads to ease this deal;
takes time and ready cash to grease
      the wheels within wheels within wheels.

The bureaucracy gets worse and worse.
      I'm stuck, like back in Aden.
I wait, watch others' camels – curse
      them leaving fully laden.

Sometimes I visit other merchants
       in their camp beneath the palms.
They post their guards with Remingtons.
         They, too, are shifting arms.

> *I authorize M. Rimbaud to take from chez*
> *Soleillet the 1000 piston rifles belonging to me.*
> *M. Rimbaud is free to sell them together or singly,*
> *but not for less than 6 thalers each. He will be*
> *glad... to take the remainder to Shoa and deliver*
> *them to M. Pino, for whom I intend them.*
> — *Labatut, 4 June 1886*

My partner Labatut fell ill
       – a tumour on the brain.
He had no choice: returned to France.
       My choice? I must remain.

I planned to join my caravan
       with that of Soleillet.
Grave news. A stroke has felled that man.
       He died the other day.

And Labatut, who was at death's door...
       – Seems now he's stepped inside.
Can't share the burden any more.
       My allies all have died.

Extortion, bribes, embargoes, lies.
       White men here don't make old bones.
The time has come to seize the prize
       – but for the thieves, I'd leave alone.

At last, I've shelled out all the bribes
       and face the trek ahead,
through burning deserts, murderous tribes,
       over men they left for dead.

Caravan to Shoa

M. Rimbaud, French trader, arrived from Tadjourah with his caravan. He has had a troublesome time of it. The same story: misconduct, greed and treachery from the men; harassment and surprise attacks from the Danakil; lack of water; the camel-drivers taking advantage.... He knows Arabic and speaks Amharic and Oromo. He is indefatigable. His aptitude for languages, his strong will and unfailing patience place him in the ranks of accomplished travellers.
—Jules Borelli, 9 February 1887

Out there, you come upon...

The remains of corpses, half-devoured
      by beasts and birds of prey;
a strip of bright-striped cloth has flowered
      to mock sun-blasted day.

Jaw-bone, picked ribs, this cracked hip-bowl;
      what pokes through rags is all bleached white.
(And that glinting tooth, I thought I saw...
      a heat-haze trick of this harsh light?
The tribes round here would leave no gold,
      but wrench your teeth from skull for sure.)

Out here, those ledgers and calculations
      suddenly require your life
be balanced by stark negotiations
      on the blade of a Danakil knife.

Not fifty, nor even sixty, days
      – for four foul months we trekked
through deserts, badlands, the dreadful glaring
      moon of Asal salt lake.

Eternities of burning plain, sterile
      miles of broken rock,
to climb the highland cool where shepherds
      tend their fat-tailed flocks.

Then finally, this Christian spot;
       three white-washed churches, round and squat:
Saints Michael, Mary, the Holy Saviour.
       Rimbaud's here. The King is not.

At the Court of the Lion of the Tribe of Judah

...there arose on every side a whole series, a whole bunch, a whole horde of creditors with stories to make your hair stand on end. This soon altered my charitable disposition. I became determined to leave Shoa as soon as possible.

— *Rimbaud, 7 April 1887*

Shoa and the times sure are a-changing:
  Ankober's had its day;
the King's new seat is now Entotto;
  the Court has moved away.

For Menelik's been waging war,
  extending his Christian domain;
Egyptians gone, he'd seized Harar.
  Hurrah! Long May He Reign!

     Hail! Hail!
   A raucous fanfare for All-Conquering King
   Menelik, Lion of the Tribe of Judah!
     Hail! Hail!
  A mighty Biblical blare on those looted Egyptian trumpets.
    Hail! Hail! He enters Entotto in triumph!
   The road judders under the King's rolling thunder:
    his spoils and his booty accompanied by
    two monstrous captured Krupp cannons,
   each hauled by eighty of the finest warriors.
     Hail! Hail!

An *azzaz* – a petty functionary
  who buzzes round the King –
bumbles up to welcome me,
  but then reveals his sting.

This toady has his donkeys ready
  – to nab what he can get.
He claims he financed Labatut
  and I must pay his debt.

Well, this *azzaz* turns out to be
　　　　some kind magistrate,
and I've made another enemy,
　　　　in this devil of a State.

What's more, it seems, he's in cahoots
　　　　with the Widow Labatut.
He's been up at Court and licking arse,
and I am caught in some terrible farce,
　　　　and now he's filed a suit.

An old Amharic proverb states:
　　　　"Beware the seeds another's sown,"
and one I learned, but far too late:
　　　　"The Master's belly is never known."

Pity the poor merchant...

Pity the poor merchant who's plying his trade,
he suffers the desert, wild tribes, bloody raids.

He kneels to the King, but he's in the wrong Court,
not summoned but summonsed by writs, edicts, torts.

This Court's a labyrinthine den
of clerks who stab with poisoned pens.

And His Royal Highness now claims he's due
huge recompense for Labatut.

(No matter that I never signed
any contract that would bind

me to his debts – even were they real.)
I'm losing big time on this deal.

These IOU's are clearly fake,
but still the King demands to take

– o machinations of the Royal Mind! –
the major part of my guns in kind

– And yes, for the rest, he gives me, *faute
de mieux* – a bloody promissory note

which I can cash when I get to Harar.
This deal gets more and more bizarre.

My money? Well, not holding my breath.
Abyssinia will be the death

of me yet. I've learned this much at least:
that I have been right royally fleeced.

Out of Entotto

...on the morning of my departure[..] I was confronted by a man who represented the wife of a friend of Labatut, who jumped out from behind a bush and demanded in the name of the Virgin Mary the sum of 19 thalers. A little further on, a creature in a sheepskin cloak leapt down from a high promontory, demanding to know if I'd paid his brother the 12 thalers Labatut had borrowed from him. I just shouted at them that they were too late.

— Rimbaud, Sunday 1 May 1887

To walk those crests of hills and breathe that air,
Oh, I was very happily out of there.
I left Entotto on the first of May
(out of the fire, or just the frying-pan?)
Borelli – conducting a survey of the route –
got Menelik's leave to join my caravan.

> *Rimbaud? Some thought his way of life grotesque,*
> *too odd and obscurely original.*
> *I liked the man, felt drawn to him.*
> *People? I take them as I find.*
> *And here was the product of an independent*
> *and rather misanthropic mind.*

... one of the nastiest tricks they can play on you in Shoa is to land you with these Orders of Payment at Harar... It is better to accept goods in Shoa, at whatever price, than payment here. These payments are tortures, disasters, tyrannies, an abominable slavery. The cash-box is in the hands of Makonnen's slaves, who behave like hydrophobic monkeys and don't let a single piastre slip out.

— Rimbaud, letter to Ilg, 20 December, 1889

At Harar I met Ras Mekonnen,
Menelik's cousin, now Governor there.
A useful contact, this *Dedjazmatch*.
We got on just fine, saw eye-to-eye.
He understands; we both have backs to scratch.
He licks his fingers, feels for further pies.

The *Labatut* business rumbles on and on.
At Aden: yet more money down the drain.
That done, it's time to get away, a break
– some R 'n' R to find my feet again.
I'll take the weekly mailboat from Steamer Point;
Red Sea up to Cairo, see how the world is getting on.

At Eritrea, the little port of Massouah:
I had some business to attend to there
– some drafts for monies to be drawn upon
from local traders (*l'affaire Labatut*
never quite seems over and finally done).
Just off the boat, when the *carabinieri*...
– long story short – arrested me.

Merciniez, French Consul here,
pops something in the diplomatic bag,
consults head office back at Aden.
Charm offensive: soon all is sorted.
The Consul's tone has changed. I'm free to go.
What's more, he's taken a shine to me:
writes letters of introduction; most usefully to
the Marquis de Grimaldi-Régusse in Cairo.

M. Rimbaud is a very honourable Frenchman, a trader and explorer in Shoa and Harar, countries he knows extremely well...

Time to go, to catch that ship.
Drop off at Suez, make contacts, friends.
So far, a very *useful* trip.

We all have good memories of your short stay at Suez, and we hope to shake you by the hand when the Gods bring you back to Egypt.
— Lucien Labosse, vice-consul, Suez

Cairo

I put up at the *Hôtel Europe*. Life here
is very much *à la européene*.
Bustling? Yes, well, seething, chaotic and dear.

Odd to be back in a big city again,
under the wobbly fan in the musty plush
with French and English papers, a cold beer.

Outside, donkeys, camels, the endless rush
of carts and business, madmen, beggars, the push
and shove of the warren, its hawkers, cheeky kids.

I leave this still-point: the eye of the storm where I sit
and think. The lobby door revolves, sun skids
on glass. Babel reels round itself: I'm hit

by the feverish synaesthesia of the street:
burning charcoal, shisha, sweat and shit.

*

Days, burdened by my money belt
– over sixteen thousand *francs d'or*,
sweating at my ribs, eight kilos and more.
At every step for weeks, it's chafed. I've felt

the golden weight of trade: its swing and shift
hanging from my bones. The *muezzin* calls:
this morning, anxious, I could have almost prayed,
depositing my future in the *Crédit Lyonnais*.

That done, I might as well go see the sights.
Outside, the pony, trap and guide await.

43

The lobby door revolves; once more sun skids
on glass. A trip to see the Pyramids.
Away from the Babel. Summer, the city stinks:
time to ponder the riddle of the Sphinx.

*

Plans

1.

I draft an article for Borelli's brother,
– editor of *Le Bosphore Égyptien.*
Scribble a proposal for another,
properly equipped, expedition;
perhaps *la Société de Géographie*
may be interested? Let's see...

2.

I have my contacts and know the game.
The future's happening. Can feel the change.
Return to Harar? – Build the business up.
Explore new routes. Link Shoa with the coast.
Four, five years more? Well, ten at most.

And then? France? Maybe Marseille.
Not Paris, somewhere by the sea.
Stay further south? Try Italy?

Those fever dreams, hallucinations
– *illuminations?* – odd visions seen.
All those futures left so long behind.
The hard terrain you sketch between
the shifting borders of map and mind.

Poetry? Ah, the very tedium.
Embrace the rugged reality:
money is the one, true medium.

Time rewards the patient, not the rash.
FOR SALE – Everything that's not been sold.
Real alchemy is turning *things* to gold.
Piss-pots, pans, tin plates, cracked bowls
all magicked, readied into cash.

La Maladie Bazardique

I suppose I've finally found my level,
back in Harar... yes, well, better the devil...
"Commission agent" for César Tian,
with several other interests on the side;
somewhere between a rep and businessman.
Truth is I'm a glorified market trader,
shifting stock cubes, slippers, macaroni,
buttons, knick-knacks, pottery, cloth, phoney
eau-de-cologne, carpets, peppermint,
hand-coloured marine and bucolic Alpine prints,
hairbrushes, ornamental oyster shells,
scissors, needles, tiny enamelled bells,
musk, gilded braid, plates, rugs, jugs, woollen coats;
skins from panther, ibex, right down to goat.

*

Some kind of madness affects us all:
the strong succumb as do the weak,
to melancholy, mania, an idée *fixe.*
Take Rimbaud's crazy market-stall
– his maladie bazardique.

*

I had some pitchers made to my design
and sold five hundred to the Ras's court,
but Makonnen has now returned them all.
I bear the risk. Again the loss is mine.
The days drag: accounts, warehouse reports.
The old rheumatism is back. Boredom. Pain.
The world shrinks to my leg, this market-stall.

*

For weeks I've felt it there,
but now it never goes away.
Those little hammer blows
inside my knee
are getting sharper by the day.

Ledgers

The years I've been here, almost always bored;
condemned to speak their gibberish, eat their filthy food.
O what a miserable existence I've endured.
I've tried to help them. Silly children! They reward
my efforts with laziness, treachery, stupidity.

So far from any intelligent society,
I fear becoming brutalized myself.
Boredom, disease, stuck south of Nowhere, the pits.
The soul dries up, or else it slowly rots;
fevers, malaria, pox, dysentery, the shits;
tobacco, booze, *quat*, quinine, tonics, pills.
To feel one's sweated one's life away... and bit
by bit one begins to think it's time to set
it down – the real double-entry ledger – the will.

*

It's like a nail's been driven in.
And now my leg is badly swollen.
I've rigged up a bed where I can lie
during the day and keep an eye
on the cash-box, ledgers, the courtyard scales.
Blink and everything is stolen.

Those years I tried to be *another*,
and now it's all come down to *me*:
a bed, a stall, this poisoned knee;
debts, goods, receipts, the endless bother;
money, boredom, and now the agony.

3. FEROCIOUS INVALID

Letters Home

Harar, 20 February 1891

Dear Mother,
Bad food, poor lodging, worries of all kinds;
natives both stupid and dishonest. I find
one ages quickly here. We whites are cursed.
There is no doctor. Daily, my leg gets worse.
(Could you send me a stocking, please?
The sort for varicose veins. They cover the knees.
For a long, thin leg, in shoe-size forty-one.)
I'll leave here soon enough... Glad to be gone.

Aden, 23 April 1891

I liquidated all, sold off the lot.
So now, I'm in the hospital. I've got
the only room for patients who can pay.
The journey overland took twelve hard days,
with my sixteen porters fully-laden,
and then the ferry across the Straits to Aden.

I try to rest and keep my sense of humour.
I have an English doctor. He fears the tumour's
reached a very serious point: too late
to save the leg. He wants to amputate.

I'll take the steamer, get home by any road.
– Another week or so the bank should cough
the thirty thousand francs I still am owed.
P. S. The stockings are useless. I'll sell them off.

Those bearers feared me: one jolt I used the rod.
My Fate: to let Disaster become my God!

Got out of Hell, and found not Eden but Aden.
(Our final voyage is always so oddly maiden!)
What lies beyond Marseilles? —and who can tell?
At night on board, I keep a lonely vigil;
right through each clanging watch, its tolling bell.

Hôpital de la Conception, Marseilles, 23 May 1891

After thirteen days at sea, arrived Marseilles.
In hospital – I pay ten francs a day
(doctors included, all in).
I'm rags on bone, a skeleton.
My leg is swollen like a pumpkin.

Marseilles, 23 June 1891

I've ceased to live. I weep both day and night.
So much was taken by that surgeon's knife.
Truth is, I'm crippled. My future's in the past.
– Farewell marriage, family, what hope of a wife?
Six months before I'll get *the leg* at last.
I'm making do with a wooden thing and stick.
        I navigate the ward by crutch,
        pajamas with one leg pinned up.

– Those other lives I thought were once our due?
You get just one. And mine is done. It's true
that this is no life. No life at all.
My stump still hurts. I stumble, sometimes fall.

And now? How all I mused just seems *unreal*.
I thought that I'd return with limbs of steel;
that women cared for these ferocious invalids.
Did I believe in saints? In their good deeds?

I'm done. I'm little more than a lopped-off tree.
However stupid his existence, man,
despite his wretched life, his misery,
he still clings on. He still clings on.
          P. S. I can't come home to you just yet.
          The cold would see me off in weeks.
          I'll come up there next month, July,
          then head back south before the autumn comes.

Marseilles, 10 July 1891

My dear Sister,
I tried the wooden leg (price 50 francs):
too sore, and only got the stump inflamed.
I've set the bloody instrument aside,
before I'm further maimed, lamed, or shamed.
For drugs, the poppy's balm, I give much thanks.

The Great Rimbaud

This time we've got it! We know where Arthur Rimbaud is, the great Rimbaud.
*the true Rimbaud, the Rimbaud of the **Illuminations**. This isn't another*
Decadent prank. We affirm it: we've found the lair of the missing poet! Traced
him to the Heart of Darkness!
— La France moderne, 19 February 1891

His mother's house, Roche, Ardennes, July–August 1891

I thought myself an Angel, Mage,
exempt from all morality.
I tried to soar, fell back to earth
to hug this gnarled reality.
(Mere craftsman, poor demi-urge,
my fire dead, my rage all purged.)

I hobble around the family plot.
I know what's near, and fear it's final.
I flittered once: a drunken gnat
in the rainbows of an inn's urinal.

Those other lives I felt my due
rise from the steam of my poppy tea:
I *was* another. Which self was true?
Who hugged his gnarled reality?

*

As he passes through Paris with Isabelle,
(the Gare de Lyons, as evening fell)
for the overnight train down to Marseilles,
in a quiet street off St Germain-des-Prés,
an editor marks the proofs he's spread.
Elsewhere, Latin Quarter literati
have just one question buzzing heads:
at tables or zinc in the right cafés,
or at a critic's dinner party,
Rimbaud — Is he alive or dead?

Harar, 12 July 1891

I have learned with astonishment that they have been obliged to cut off your leg. According to what you have told me the operation was a success. God be praised! I learn with pleasure that you are proposing to come back to Harar to continue with your business: that gives me pleasure. Yes, come back soon in good health. I am still your friend. — *Ras Makonnen*

Delirium

Hôpital de la Conception, Marseilles, 9-10 November 1891

I dreamed the army had caught up with me,
for the National Service I still owed.
Press-ganged, I squarebashed with some kids.
The drill was hard. Worse still parades.
There were my legs, now one, now three,
but never quite the pair required.
I must escape. Get to the port.
It is night. I hear the ship's bell ring.

He is delirious, whole hours he babbles;
his mind is full of strange itineraries.
Last night he raved about returning east,
booking passage on the Aphinar.
I have made enquires in the port,
and from an old sea-captain who visits here;
there is no such vessel, I am assured.

Last Rites

A priest's been summoned by Isabelle,
with all the sacred impedimenta.
He hovers to hold me back from Hell.
Been there before. Am I slipping back,
spiralling down to the Dantean centre?
Once did that trek, since covered my tracks.

What good is this? These Rites, my last?
Forget Communion, or Confession.
Forgive me, Father: no intercession!
Not even God can change the past.

This life is pain, disappointment, grief.
This priest, peddling Salvation, God,
requires the suspension of Disbelief.
I'm earth to earth, just sod to sod.
O, ever since the damned Year Dot,
we've all gone from life, its strange mishaps,
like Voltaire, towards a great Perhaps... or Not.

I am the poet's sister Isabelle:
my brother has been spared from Hell!
Arthur surprised us with his piety.
He died in Christ and will live forever! PRAISE BE!

Obsequies

1.   *Charleville, several days later*

No one invited, no one came.
No notice in the local press.
A hungry dog, half-blind and lame,
the hired hands in mourning dress;

the priest, gravedigger, undertaker,
the deaf mute brought to ring the bell,
some text, some verse, some "Meet thy Maker,"
four cantors, Maman, Isabelle.

He'll lie inside the family vault,
with newly-chiselled name and dates.
Maman is grim. She bred his faults:
the iron pride clanged shut like gates.

The cemetery light is growing dim.
The shadows gather in the grove:
that stony incisive *Pray for him*
already blunting in the groove.

2.   *Verlaine, Café Procope, Paris*

He was my one "great radiant sin."
I lost my wife, my only son.
The things we do for skin on skin,
all over now. What's done is done.

Here I remain, an old bent Gent,
a drunken "Immortal" among the whores.
I wrote some verse, less good than meant.
My other sins were small for sure.

A hopeless bugger, a weak arsehole,
I did my time, took my punishment.
Sometimes I think he stole my soul,
but my great sin stays radiant.
And I'll be damned, if I'll repent.

Reliquary

Verlaine, Paris, some months later

1.

Did he have some secret for changing life?
I see his name now everywhere:
all Paris gossips, speculation's rife.

Suddenly, *Le Reliquaire*,
that bad edition of his verse, appeared
the day *L'Echo* announced his death.

Some sort of quarrel; that book withdrawn.
"Other horrible workers will come," *he* said:
they'll mourn, and butcher the boy who's dead.

I did the job. They take me for a fool:
new poems appear, the ones he did not write;
now Seraph of the "Decadent-Symbolist School",
he was no Angel, my clever little shite.

2.

As a career move, his death has served him well.
The writing began and ended, I know, with me.
Where would he be now (apart from Hell?)
without my guide to *Les Poètes Maudits*?

3.

His sister, goody-two-shoes Isabelle,
says that she "wants to put the record straight."
Came to see me. That self-righteous bitch
claimed that at the end "he saw the Light
and went to Jesus." Jesus! That Catholic witch.

She paints a sinner turned unlikely saint.
I'm sure the hagiography is planned.
She'll tidy him up. Purify his soul.
She's after letters, anything in his hand.
(She'd burn *Zutiques*, put our lewdness to Hell's fire.)
The way she speaks of *him*! She's found her rôle:
a sanctimonious, revisionist liar.
A whitewashed sepulchre: his name will glow
in golden script: *Le Tombeau de Rimbaud*.

Le Tombeau de Rimbaud

*I have learned of the death of M. Arthur Rimbaud. He is better known
in France as a decadent poet than as a traveller, but under the latter title
he also deserves to be remembered.*
— *Alfred Bardey, letter read to the Société de Géographie, 22 January 1892*

Charleville

From Africa to right back there,
the birthplace that he loved to hate;
his monument surveys the square,
courtesy: *the admiring State.*

The Master of Silence looks out, not down
– a chess-piece bust, no verse, no rants –
municipal above the town,
above the council bedding plants.

The kid who mocked the Poet's flowers
has bloomed in school anthologies;
he sang his Song from the Highest Tower,
then the Seer climbed down, fled overseas.

Forever seventeen he stares
his future out from Charleville.
He knows the roads that knot this square,
the lanes beyond whose ruts break wheels,
      the tenant farms where lives get stuck,
      the cankered crop, the used-up luck.

Reverb

les tombeaux de Rimbaud

1.

No, not the one in your home town
    of Charleville-Mezières.
Not graveyard, nor the monument,
    that bust in the park just off the square.

Not the museum by the Meuse
    – the river tourists call "the Muse" –
your fan-mail gets delivered where
    aspirant poets still pay their dues.

On others it seems decay has smiled,
    and when it comes to Death's des res,
Mister Mojo Risin' and Oscar Wilde
    are chilling down at Père Lachaise.

But, dusted off, you're everywhere:
from page to stage, through screen, on air.

*

2.

You ended up as *someone else*
    (no riches, peace, no dark-skinned wife);
your printed past parenthesized
    by the margins of your After-Life.

From modernist *avant la lettre*,
    to immortally dead celebrity,
you razored down your *raison d'être*
    to business-minded amputee.

You said enough, then held your tongue.
        Master of Silence? or acting dumb?
You broke the lyric, tore up the song.
        Saw other horrible workers come.

The hypertext escapes the ink;
ghosts behind the glowing link.

*

3.

Whose lines can ever outlast bronze?
        Though your brassy voice outlasted you.
You must have weighed the pros and cons,
        ex-Hooligan-Seer, Voyant-Voyou.

We turn to ash and bone so fast,
        from Genesis to Revelation.
Not even God can change the past.
        You catch some chance illumination.

The lightning forks, the road does too.
        You make your choice by the sudden light.
You hope your stars, your path, were true.
        No more painted words, just black and white.

Whose song can ever outlast bronze?
You hear it. Now the tongue is gone.

Commemorative plaque Hôpital de la Conception, Marseille

ICI

LE 10 NOVEMBRE 1891 REVENANT D'ADEN
LE POÈTE JEAN ARTHUR RIMBAUD
RENCONTRA LA FIN
DE SON AVENTURE TERRESTRE

Acknowledgments

This poem draws on material from many sources; the following books were particularly useful.

Charles Nicholl, *Somebody Else: Arthur Rimbaud in Africa 1880-91*, Jonathan Cape 1991

Graham Robb, *Rimbaud*, Picador 2000

eds Jeremy Harding and John Sturrock, *Arthur Rimbaud: Selected Poems and Letters*, Penguin Classics, 2004

A short essay on writing this sequence "Reversifying Rimbaud" appeared on the Royal Literary Fund showcase:
https://www.rlf.org.uk/showcase/reversifying-rimbaud/

LAY OUT YOUR UN:REST

www.ingramcontent.com/pod-product-compliance
Lightning Source LLC
Chambersburg PA
CBHW021940040426
42448CB00008B/1160